THE
LAST TRA

(2) Glasgow & Centra Scotland

Edited by W. S. Sellar & J. L. Stevenson

W. S. Sellar

One of the last excursion trains to leave Glasgow (Buchanan Street) prepares for departure for Aberdeen behind A4 No 60019 *Bittern* on September 3rd 1966. The station closed completely on November 7th 1966.

MOORFOOT PUBLISHING
EDINBURGH

This collection of photographs attempts to record the last trains on closed lines in Glasgow and the counties of Dunbartonshire, Lanarkshire, Renfrewshire, and West Lothian. 'Last Trains' are not rigidly defined in this booklet—some illustrations show regular passenger trains on or around the closure date, others illustrate specially-chartered trains operated after closure. If readers have photographs of rail services omitted from this booklet, the publisher would be happy to hear from them.

The opening of Glasgow's Argyle line in 1979 using much of the closed Central Low Level system proves that abandoned railways may still hold the solution to transport problems of the future. It is particularly appropriate that a city like Glasgow, which has always been associated with the development of the railway industry, should witness the reinvigoration of urban railways. Hopefully, the 'Last Trains' series can assist this development in some small way by reminding the Scottish public of transport options available in the past.

Series note—Volume 1 of this series was published in July 1979 and records the last trains on withdrawn services in Edinburgh and south-east Scotland. The next issue, volume 3, will cover south-west Scotland, and national coverage will be completed in due course.

Erratum: In volume 1, please note that the photograph of locomotive No 43129 on the Riccarton-Hexham line was taken on November 9th 1963, and not in 1956 as the caption unintentionally implied.

Acknowledgments: Thanks are due to all photographers and picture archives whose assistance was invaluable in producing this booklet. Photographic credits are given alongside the pictures. Supplementary information was provided by R. Hamilton, R. Montgomery, and the Mitchell Library, Glasgow.

Moorfoot Publishing
PO Box 506
SW Postal District
Edinburgh 10

ISBN 0 906606 02 0

Printed by Macdonald Printers (Edinburgh) Ltd., Edgefield Road, Loanhead, Midlothian

W.S. Sellar

Glasgow (Townhead) 1849

No cameras were available in 1849 to record the last train at the Glasgow and Garnkirk Railway terminus at Glasgow (Townhead). The station closed to passengers when the company was absorbed by the Caledonian Railway which opened Buchanan Street station in that year. J37 No 64623 poses on the station site with a surviving G. & G. R. building in the background, on March 27th 1964.

Horse-drawn passenger services began on the Monkland & Kirkintilloch Railway as far back as 1828 but by 1850 the system had reverted to mineral haulage, its staple traffic. On April 2nd 1966 diesel shunter No D2736 hauled the last train from Kirkintilloch (Basin), seen here at Whitegates.

Monkland Railway 1850

D. Martin

W. A. C. Smith

Potterhill 1917

This G.S.W.R. branch from Paisley (West) lost its passenger service on January 1st 1917 although retained for freight for more than a further half-century. The lower end was used for rounding passenger trains terminating at Paisley (West) and 0-6-0 No 57241 is seen performing this operation on April 27th 1957.

The hospital at Bangour (West Lothian) was formerly served by a little-known branch from Uphall and worked by the N.B.R. until closure on May 4th 1921. An N.B.R. 2-4-0 stands on a passenger train at Bangour terminus.

Bangour 1921

Royal Commission on Ancient Monuments, Scotland

J. L. Stevenson

Govan 1921

This short branch from Ibrox, part of the Glasgow and Paisley Joint line, lost its passenger service on May 9th 1921 but was occasionally used by excursion trains, or, as here, by a rail tour headed by former C. R. class 60 4-6-0, No 54634, on May 3rd 1952.

This sparsely-used line lasted only until July 14th 1924. The intermediate halt at Calderwood Glen, unfortunately shown minus train, is a long-vanished reminder.

East Kilbride-Hamilton 1924

Lens of Sutton

W. S. Sellar

Renfrew (Porterfield) 1926

The Glasgow and Paisley Joint branch from Cardonald lost its passenger service on July 19th 1926 but remained open for freight. A brake van tour with 0-6-0 No 57689 reached Porterfield on March 23rd 1963. The line to Renfrew Wharf is in the foreground.

The branch from Bathgate to Blackston Junction, where it connected with the straggling Manuel-Coatbridge line, lost its passenger service on May 1st 1930. The last rail tour on the line, hauled by preserved D34 No 256 *Glen Douglas,* is pictured crossing the river Almond between Westfield and Blackston on June 19th 1962.

Bathgate-Blackston Junction 1930

W. A. C. Smith

J. L. Stevenson

Manuel-Coatbridge 1930
Passenger services ceased from May 1st 1930 on this steeply graded line. Rail tours continued to operate over some of the remaining sections and former C. R. 4-4-0 No 54465 is seen at Bowhouse in May 1960 with the two preserved C. R. coaches.

Passenger services on this line ceased on May 1st 1930, but much of the line was retained for freight and on May 6th 1961 carried a rail tour, hauled by N15 No 69163. It is shown at what was then the terminus from Bathgate, Fauldhouse and Crofthead.
Morningside (LNER)-Bathgate 1930

J. L. Stevenson

W. S. Sellar

Airdrie-Newhouse 1930

Passenger services on this line were withdrawn on December 1st 1930, but a rail tour powered by 0-6-0 No 57581 visited Newhouse on June 9th 1962, having travelled from Bellside Junction, Cleland.

Closed to passenger traffic on December 1st 1930, the LMSR station was situated at the site of an end-on connection with the rather similar LNER station seen in the background.

Morningside (LMSR)-Holytown 1930

Professor Fordyce

G. E. Langmuir

Balloch-Stirling 1934

The former Forth and Clyde Railway was closed to passenger traffic on October 1st 1934 although the central section continued to carry the Aberfoyle service until 1951. In the last years passenger services between Balloch and Stirling were mainly worked by Sentinel railcars, one of which, *Quicksilver,* is seen at Balloch in the 1930s.

The passenger service to this eastern extremity of the Glasgow Central Low Level system was cut back to Whifflet on May 3rd 1943. A rail tour train is shown awaiting departure at Airdrie behind 0-6-0 No 57581 on June 9th 1962.

Airdrie-Langloan 1943

J. L. Stevenson

G. E. Langmuir

Bothwell (Caledonian) 1950

Leaving the Glasgow (Central)—Carlisle main line at Fallside just east of Uddingston, this branch, only one mile in length, had an infrequent service. An 0-4-4 tank engine is shown at the terminus, which boasted an overall roof for most of its life. The branch closed completely on June 5th 1950.

This was the terminus of a branch from Jordanhill and was one of the former NBR's western suburban termini. Passenger services were withdrawn on April 2nd 1951 and two V1s are illustrated working trains in the last week of service.

Whiteinch (Victoria Park) 1951

G. H. Robin

G. H. Robin

Kilsyth-Maryhill 1951
The route between Glasgow (Maryhill) and Kilsyth via Torrance had latterly only one train daily in each direction. C15 No 67480 is shown bringing one of these into Kilsyth in July 1950. This service ceased on April 2nd 1951.

V1 No 67664 leaves the Aberfoyle line at Kelvin Valley West Junction with a train from Glasgow (Queen Street) on July 30th 1951, a week before the withdrawal of the service.
Kilsyth-Lenzie 1951

G. H. Robin

J. L. Stevenson

Paisley-Barrhead

Built by the Caledonian Railway at the turn of the century with full passenger facilities this line was used only for freight. The first and last passenger train, a rail tour worked by 0-6-0 No 57266, calls at Glenfield station on September 1st 1951.

Although worked for a time by Sentinel railcars, operations had reverted to locomotive haulage by May 1948 when C15 No 7475 headed a train at the terminus. The service ceased from September 10th 1951.

Hamilton (LNER)-Blairhill & Gartsherrie 1951

J. L. Stevenson

J. L. Stevenson

Wilsontown 1951
0-6-0 No 57438 prepares to work the branch train to Carstairs on September 8th 1951, the last day of passenger operation.

Even on the last day, September 29th 1951, a single coach sufficed for the Aberfoyle passenger service. The branch train is seen here at Blane Valley Junction, Lennoxtown, behind J37 No 64639.
Aberfoyle 1951

G. H. Robin

J. L. Stevenson collection

Brocketsbrae 1951

Once busy with coal traffic, this branch from Hamilton became something of a backwater and lost its passenger service on October 1st 1951. 0-4-4 tank engine No 55182 stands on a single coach train to Hamilton on the penultimate day of service.

Closure of the Hamilton-Bothwell section of this line took place on September 15th 1952 owing to the condition of the Clyde viaduct. On the last day V1 No 67648 awaits departure from Hamilton.

Hamilton (LNER)-Shettleston 1952

W. A. C. Smith

W. S. Sellar

Bothwell (LNER)-Shettleston 1955
From 1952 to 1955 Bothwell was the terminus of the former NBR line from Shettleston to Hamilton. On July 2nd 1955, the very day of closure, V3 No 67678 prepares to leave Bothwell for Hyndland.

Passenger services between Airdrie and Edinburgh (Waverley) via Bathgate ceased on January 9th 1956. J35 No 64468 is seen passing Polkemmet Junction, Bathgate, with a train for Hyndland on the last day (see also cover).
Bathgate 1956

G. H. Robin

W. A. C. Smith

Bo'ness 1956

This short branch, leaving the Edinburgh-Glasgow main line two miles east of Polmont, closed to passenger traffic on May 7th 1956. 4MT No 43141 was working on the last day at Bo'ness.

The G.S.W.R. line to Greenock lost its regular passenger service beyond Kilmacolm on February 2nd 1959 but carried Ocean Liner specials for a time thereafter. 2-6-4 tank engine No 42268 leaves Princes Pier on the last day of scheduled services.

Greenock (Princes Pier) 1959

W. A. C. Smith

J. L. Stevenson

Clydebank (East) 1959

This was one of the western termini of the North Clyde suburban system, located at the end of a short spur. It was closed on September 14th 1959. N2 No 69507 heads a train here in February 1955.

The Kirklee line through Kelvinbridge lost its passenger services on November 23rd 1959, five years before the rest of the Low Level system. The three intermediate stations on the line had been closed earlier. 2-6-4 tank engine No 42689 is seen passing Kelvinbridge in October 1959 before the end of passenger operations.

Glasgow (Central Low Level)-Kirklee 1959

J. L. Stevenson

G. H. Robin

Hyndland 1960

This terminus, at the end of a short spur from Partickhill, was closed on October 5th 1960 concurrently with electrification and was replaced by a new through station on the main line. V1 No 67665 enters with a train on April 30th 1960.

2-6-4 tank No 42246 worked the last train on March 31st 1962. Thereafter services terminated at Neilston (High) which shortly afterwards became part of the electrified network.

Uplawmoor 1962

Hamish Stevenson

W. A. C. Smith

Glasgow (Buchanan Street)-Hamilton 1962
One of Buchanan Street's services to cease before the closure of the terminus itself was the Hamilton service, with various short workings. 2-6-4 tank No 42208 is seen on the final day of operation on November 3rd 1962 at Mossend, this being the last train to call.

The Singer sewing machine company boasted a private terminus for its staff just south of the main line where the present Singer station is located. V1 No 67602 is seen at the terminus on December 10th 1960. Electric trains used the terminus until its closure on March 2nd 1964.
Singer (Works) 1964

W. A. C. Smith

J. L. Stevenson

Kirkintilloch 1964

The 1½ mile Kirkintilloch branch from Lenzie remained after the withdrawal of the Aberfoyle and Kilsyth services until it too was closed, on September 7th 1964. At the end of the final week NBL Type 2 diesels D6120 and D6105 brought in a train from Glasgow (Queen Street).

The passenger service between Langloan and Whifflet (Upper) lasted until October 3rd 1964 when it shared the fate of the rest of the Glasgow (Central Low Level) lines. A DMU stands at Whifflet (Upper) on the last morning prior to working to Maryhill (Central).

Airdrie-Langloan (II) 1964

Hamish Stevenson

W. A. C. Smith

Glasgow (Central Low Level Lines) (I) 1964

The former Caledonian Low Level network was closed from October 3rd 1964 but happily the principal section was reopened as the Argyle Line with electric traction fifteen years later. On the final day 4MT No 76074 stands at Dalmuir Riverside ready to work the last train through to Rutherglen.

The network's northern section through Maryhill to Possil also closed on this date. 2-6-4 tank No 42203 stands in a dock at the large station at Maryhill (Central) in 1959.

Glasgow (Central Low Level Lines) (II) 1964

W. S. Sellar

W. A. C. Smith

Coalburn 1965
Running mainly parallel with the Brocketsbrae line, this fared better in retaining its passenger services from Hamilton until October 4th 1965. On the final day a DMU enters Stonehouse while the signalman waits to exchange the tablet.

The short branch between Strathaven and Stonehouse on the Coalburn line closed simultaneously with the latter on October 4th 1965. A feature was the twin viaducts at Strathaven where 2-6-4 tank No 42164 is seen approaching in July 1953. In the background is the viaduct carrying the Blantyre line which lost its passenger services on September 30th 1945.
Strathaven 1965

G. H. Robin

J. L. Stevenson

Glasgow (St Enoch) 1966

The splendid G.S.W.R. terminus was closed on June 27th 1966 and ten years later razed to the ground. In the final month 4MT No 76093 heads a relief to Ayr, one of the last steam workings.

The city's northern terminus was closed from November 7th 1966 with remaining services transferred to Queen Street. B1 No 61407 banks a train as far as the tunnel-mouth a week before closure.

Glasgow (Buchanan Street) 1966

J. L. Stevenson

J. L. Stevenson

Renfrew (Wharf) 1967

This service was regularly steam-worked almost until the final withdrawal of passenger services on June 5th 1967. 2-6-4 tank No 80004 is seen shunting the empty stock of a morning train at the Wharf a few weeks before the end.

This city terminus on a branch from High Street was closed on November 5th 1979, concurrently with the opening of the Argyle Line. The photograph shows electric units in service at Bridgeton two days before closure.

Bridgeton (Central) 1979

J. L. Stevenson.